NATIONAL BASKETBALL ASSOCIATION SUPERSTARS 2005

By John Smallwood Jr.

Scholastic Inc.

New York   Toronto   London   Auckland   Sydney
Mexico City   New Delhi   Hong Kong   Buenos Aires

ISBN 0-439-70400-6

12 11 10 9 8 7 6 5 4 3   5 6 7 8/ 0

Printed in the U.S.A.
First printing, February 2005

They are the most exciting athletes in the world. More than any other sport, basketball allows its players to display their speed, grace and athleticism.

The players in the National Basketball Association are so good at what they do that sometimes their games look more like works of art than sporting events, and they look more like entertainers than athletes.

Like Houdini, a player like New Jersey Nets point guard Jason Kidd will mystify us with crossover dribbles and magical no-look passes.

Like Robin Hood, sharpshooters like Seattle SuperSonics guard Ray Allen or Dallas Mavericks forward Dirk Nowitzki will amaze us with the incredible accuracy of their long-range jumpers.

Like Superman, an athletic big man like Miami Heat forward Shaquille O'Neal will thrill us as he seemingly walks on air to make a mighty slam dunk.

For more than 50 years, the players of the NBA have thrilled us with their wondrous abilities — each generation taking the game to a new level of excitement.

But some stars shine brighter than others. These superstars play the game with a flair that sets them apart from others.

Let's meet some of them.

RAY ALLEN

GUARD
SEATTLE SUPERSONICS

BORN: 7/20/1975

HEIGHT: 6-5

WEIGHT: 205

SCHOOL: CONNECTICUT

THE NATURAL

Watching Ray Allen play basketball is watching poetry in motion. Everything the Seattle Sonics guard does he does effortlessly. Every move he makes, every shot he takes, is done smoothly and flawlessly.

Leaving the University of Connecticut after his junior season, Ray was part of the great 1996 NBA Draft, which also included Allen Iverson, Stephon Marbury, Shareef Abdur-Rahim, Kobe Bryant, and Jermaine O'Neal.

Ray was originally drafted by Minnesota but was immediately traded to the Milwaukee Bucks for Stephon Marbury. In Milwaukee, Ray became a four-time All-Star. He is still the Bucks' all-time leader in three-pointers made (1,051) and attempted (2,587); and ranks in the top ten in points (9,681 - 8th) and games (496 - 9th).

After playing the first six years of his career with the Milwaukee Bucks, Ray was traded to the Seattle SuperSonics late in the 2002–03 season. The Sonics were looking to change direction and saw Ray and his silky-smooth style as what they wanted to build around.

Ray finished the season averaging 24.0 points in 29 games as a Sonic. Because of injuries, Ray played only 56 games last season, but he still averaged 20.2 points and 4.0 assists. With Ray leading the way, the Sonics are improving and should soon be a team to watch out for.

In addition to his regular season play, Ray was a member of the 2000 United States gold-medal team at the Sydney Olympics.

DID YOU KNOW?

Ray is the NBA spokesman for the Thurgood Marshall Scholarship Fund.

ALLEN BY THE NUMBERS▷ 2003–04 SEASON POINTS: 23.0 – REBOUNDS: 5.10 – ASSISTS: 4.8 – STEALS: 1.27

CARMELO ANTHONY

FORWARD

DENVER NUGGETS

BORN: 5/29/1984
HEIGHT: 6-8
WEIGHT: 220
SCHOOL: SYRACUSE

MELO

After averaging 22.2 points and 10.0 rebounds, being named the 2003 NCAA Freshman of the Year, and leading Syracuse University to its first NCAA Championship, Carmelo Anthony could make a strong argument that he was the best player in the 2003 NBA Draft. But everyone was talking about high school sensation LeBron James as the likely No. 1 pick.

The day of the draft, Carmelo wasn't first. Nor was he drafted second. When the third pick in the draft came up, however, the Denver Nuggets made sure Carmelo would be going to the Mile High City.

That was okay with Carmelo because it just made him more determined to prove he was the best. Twenty years earlier in 1983, Michael Jordan wasn't drafted until third and then turned around the fortunes of the Chicago Bulls. Carmelo might have the same impact for the Nuggets. Carmelo became an instant superstar, leading all rookie scorers by averaging 21.0 points and helping the Nuggets improve their victory total from 17 to 43 and make the playoffs for the first time since 1995. In his first playoff appearance, Carmelo averaged 15.0 points and 8.3 rebounds.

Carmelo finished second in the got milk? Rookie of the Year voting, was named a First-Team All-Rookie Team choice, and continued his outstanding debut season by being named to the 2004 United States Olympic Team.

DID YOU KNOW?

Carmelo was named the Most Outstanding Player of the 2003 NCAA Final Four after totalling 53 points and 24 rebounds in two games.

ANTHONY BY THE NUMBERS ▷ 2003-04 SEASON POINTS: 21.0 – REBOUNDS: 6.1 – ASSISTS: 2.8

TIM DUNCAN

FORWARD/CENTER
SAN ANTONIO SPURS

BORN: 7/20/1975
HEIGHT: 7-0
WEIGHT: 260
SCHOOL: WAKE FOREST

THE BIG FUNDAMENTAL

By now the story is the stuff of legend. In 1989, Tim Duncan, then just 13 years old, was a promising swimming prospect in the 400 meters for the U.S. Virgin Islands. His older sister, Tricia, had competed in the 100- and 200-meter backstroke at the 1988 Seoul Olympics.

But on September 17, 1989, Hurricane Hugo struck Tim's home island of St. Croix and destroyed, among other things, the Olympic-size swimming pool where Tim and his sister trained, the only one on the island.

Tim soon gave up swimming and took up basketball. The rest is history. Instead of becoming the tallest Olympic swimmer, Tim became an All-American center at Wake Forest University and in 1997 was drafted first overall by the San Antonio Spurs.

After being named NBA Rookie of the Year, Tim led the Spurs to their first NBA Championship in just his second season. In 2003, he led the Spurs to a second title.

One of the most accomplished players in the world, Tim may not be flashy but he is remarkably consistent. A two-time regular season and NBA Finals MVP, Tim has averaged between 21.1 and 25.5 points, and 11.4 and 12.9 rebounds in each of his seven seasons.

Tim missed the 2000 Olympics because of injury but starred for the United States at the 2004 Olympics in Athens. The most fundamentally sound big man in the game, Tim is sure to win more titles before he is done.

DID YOU KNOW?

That in 1998 Tim became the first rookie since Larry Bird in 1979–80 to be named First-Team All-NBA.

DUNCAN BY THE NUMBERS: 2003–04 SEASON: POINTS: 22.3 – REBOUNDS: 12.4 – BLOCKS: 2.68

KEVIN GARNETT

FORWARD
MINNESOTA TIMBERWOLVES

BORN: 5/19/1976

HEIGHT: 6-11

WEIGHT: 220

SCHOOL: FARRAGUT ACADEMY HIGH SCHOOL (CHICAGO, ILLINOIS)

DA KID TO DA MAN

Before Kevin declared for the 1995 NBA Draft, no high school player had directly entered the league in 20 years. In the nine years since he joined the NBA, Garnett has gone from a 19-year-old prodigy to one of the top five players in the world.

He is a seven-time All-Star and six-time All-NBA selection (and counting). Last season, Kevin was chosen as the 2003-2004 Most Valuable Player. He was the only unanimous choice for All-NBA First-Team and was All-Defensive First Team. He also led the league in rebounding.

Falling in the first-round the previous seven seasons, Kevin and the Minnesota Timberwolves advanced all the way to the 2004 Western Conference Finals.

Now with Kevin, the player everyone once called "Da Kid," showing everyone that he has become "Da Man," there is a good chance that an NBA Championship could be coming to Minnesota in the near future.

DID YOU KNOW?

Kevin was a member of the 2000 United States gold-medal team at the Sydney Olympics and portrayed Hall of Fame center Wilt Chamberlain in the movie *Rebound*.

GARNETT BY THE NUMBERS ▶ 2003–04 SEASON: POINTS: 24.2 – REBOUNDS: 13.9 – ASSISTS: 5.0 – BLOCKS: 2.17

ALLEN IVERSON

GUARD

PHILADELPHIA 76ers

BORN: 6/7/1975
HEIGHT: 6-0
WEIGHT: 165
SCHOOL: GEORGETOWN

LITTLE BIG MAN

It's often been said that basketball is a big man's game, but Allen Iverson proves that is not always true. Barely 6-feet tall and weighing less than 165 pounds, Allen is one of the smallest players in the NBA, but in his first eight seasons, he has proven that he is one of the best.

After being selected No.1 overall by the Philadelphia 76ers in the 1996 Draft, Allen averaged 23.5 points and was named NBA Rookie of the Year.

Since then, Allen has won three scoring titles and twice averaged more than 30 points a game. He became the first player to lead the NBA in steals for three straight seasons.

During the 2000–01 season, he averaged 31.1 points and led the Sixers to the NBA Finals. Allen won the Maurice Podoloff Trophy as the NBA Most Valuable Player.

A perennial NBA All-Star, and one of the most popular players in the world, Allen made his Olympic debut playing for the United States at the 2004 Games in Athens, Greece.

With his incredible scoring ability, Allen still hopes to one day lead the Sixers to a NBA title.

DID YOU KNOW?

Allen, whose nickname is "The Answer," is the shortest MVP in NBA history.

IVERSON BY THE NUMBERS: 2003–04 SEASON: POINTS: 26.4 – ASSISTS: 6.8 – REBOUNDS: 3.7 – STEALS: 2.4

LeBRON JAMES

GUARD

CLEVELAND CAVALIERS

BORN: 12/30/1984

HEIGHT: 6-8

WEIGHT: 240

SCHOOL: ST. VINCENT-ST. MARY HIGH SCHOOL (AKRON, OHIO)

THE CHOSEN ONE

No player has entered the NBA with as much fanfare as LeBron James.

Before he began his senior year of high school in Akron, Ohio, LeBron was on the cover of *Sports Illustrated* magazine and was being called the best high school player ever. There was no doubt that after he graduated from high school, LeBron would enter the NBA Draft. In 2004, he was drafted first overall by the Cleveland Cavaliers. Before he had played a game, LeBron was called the next Michael Jordan and had signed a lucrative contract with Nike.

But if he ever felt any pressure from all of the expectations, LeBron never showed it. He simply went out and proved that everything being said about him was true, and then some.

Just 18 when he began his NBA career, LeBron averaged 20.9 points, 5.9 assists, 5.5 rebounds and 1.65 steals to earn got milk? Rookie of the Year honors. He helped the Cavaliers double their victory total from 17 to 35.

Despite being the youngest player in the NBA, LeBron was picked to play for the United States at the 2004 Olympics in Athens.

King James has arrived, and the world is watching.

DID YOU KNOW?

That LeBron also played football until his senior year and was a first-team All-State wide receiver as a sophomore.

JAMES BY THE NUMBERS◊ 2003-04 SEASON: POINTS: 20.9 – REBOUNDS: 5.5 – ASSISTS: 5.9 – STEALS: 1.65

JASON KIDD

POINT GUARD
NEW JERSEY NETS

BORN: 3/23/1973
HEIGHT: 6-4
WEIGHT: 212
SCHOOL: UNIVERSITY OF CALIFORNIA (BERKELEY)

MASTER AND COMMANDER

He is the best in the NBA at what he does. And what Jason Kidd does best is make other players better. A blend of old school and new school, Jason has become the prototype for the modern point guard. He is an unselfish play-creator who can turn into a playmaker in the single bounce of a ball. With his ability to pass, rebound, and score, Jason is a threat to have a triple-double in any given game.

A natural leader, Jason uses his uncanny court-vision to orchestrate a symphony of motion on the basketball court. An inch of space is all he needs to make the perfect pass to a teammate to finish a play.

A four-time All-NBA First Team selection, Jason is only the fourth player to lead the league in assists for three straight seasons. He became the sixth fastest player to reach 5,000 by doing so in 531 games.

After being traded to the New Jersey Nets in 2001, Jason joined a team that had been to the playoffs just once since 1994 and led them to the NBA Finals. In 2003, he had the Nets back in the Finals.

A member of the United States 2000 gold-medal team, Jason is still the best all-around point guard in the game.

DID YOU KNOW?
Every Christmas, Jason and his wife, Joumana, take kids from a local shelter on a shopping spree at a toy store.

KIDD BY THE NUMBERS > 2003–04 SEASON: POINTS: 15.5 – ASSISTS: 9.2 – REBOUNDS: 6.4

STEPHON MARBURY

BORN: 2/20/1977
HEIGHT: 6-2
WEIGHT: 205
SCHOOL: GEORGIA TECH

THE PRODIGAL GUARD

The way Stephon Marbury tells it, he was born to be a point guard. Growing up as a schoolboy legend in New York City, Stephon always wanted to play for the hometown Knicks.

After playing for three teams in his first seven seasons, Stephon's dream came true when, midway through the 2003–04 season he was traded from the Phoenix Suns to the Knicks. Raised in the Coney Island section of Brooklyn, Stephon hadn't been born the last time that the Knicks won an NBA title, but he is determined to help turn things around.

In 47 games with the Knicks, Stephon averaged 19.8 points and 9.3 assists. He helped the team reach the playoffs for the first time in two seasons.

Last season, Stephon was the only player in the NBA to rank in the top 15 in points and assists. A two-time NBA All-Star, Stephon was a member of the 2004 United States Olympic team.
Now Stephon wants to help lead the Knicks to that long-awaited NBA Championship.

DID YOU KNOW?

Stephon and Hall of Fame guard Oscar Robertson are the only players in NBA history with more than a 20 points and 8 assists career average.

MARBURY BY THE NUMBERS◊ 2003–04 SEASON: POINTS: 20.2 – ASSISTS: 8.9 – REBOUNDS: 3.2 – STEALS: 1.59

TRACY McGRADY

GUARD
HOUSTON ROCKETS

BORN: 5/24/1979
HEIGHT: 6-8
WEIGHT: 210
SCHOOL: MT. ZION CHRISTIAN ACADEMY (North Carolina)

T-MAC

When it comes to scoring, only a handful of players can do it as well as Tracy McGrady.

Last season, the Orlando Magic finished with the worst record in the league, but T-Mac won his second straight scoring title, averaging 28.0 points.

While some questioned whether Tracy was ready for the NBA when he declared for the 1997 Draft out of high school, it only took a few years to prove his doubters wrong. Originally drafted by the Toronto Raptors, Tracy came to the Orlando Magic after the 1999–2000 season to escape the shadow of his distant cousin Vince Carter.

With the Magic, Tracy averaged a career-high 26.8 points. But after four seasons with little playoff success in Orlando, Tracy decided it was time to try his fortunes elsewhere.

In one of the biggest trades in the league, Orlando moved Tracy and Juwan Howard, Tyronn Lue, and Reece Gaines to the Houston Rockets for All-Star guard Steve Francis, guard Cuttino Mobley, and center Kelvin Cato. Teamed with center Yao Ming, Tracy thinks he can finally achieve team success to go with his individual success. "I'm just looking forward to something great happening in Houston," Tracy said, "and trust me, something great is going to happen."

In 2002–03, Tracy dethroned Allen Iverson to win his first scoring title. Now in Houston, T-Mac is looking to add a NBA title to his scoring ones.

DID YOU KNOW?

When Tracy finished the 2002–03 campaign as the NBA scoring champion by averaging 32.1 points, he became the youngest player to average 30-plus points per game since the NBA absorbed four ABA teams prior to the merger in 1976–77 and the youngest since Bob McAdoo (34.5) in 1974–75.

McGRADY BY THE NUMBERS〉 2003–04 SEASON: POINTS: 28.0 – REBOUNDS: 6.0 STEALS: 1.39 – ASSISTS: 5.5

YAO MING
CENTER
HOUSTON ROCKETS

BORN: 9/12/1980

HEIGHT: 7-5

WEIGHT: 296

SCHOOL: SHANGHAI PHYSICAL & SPORT TECHNIC EDUCATION INSTITUTE

THE MING DYNASTY

Yao Ming wasn't the first player from China to enter the NBA. In fact, he was the third. But in two seasons, he has unquestionably had the biggest impact. In 2002, the Houston Rockets made Yao the first player from an international league to be drafted first overall. He immediately became one of the most recognizable and marketable athletes in the world.

But Yao proved to be much more than just a name. As a rookie he won the voting to start at center for the Western Conference in the NBA All-Star Game, coming in ahead of former Los Angeles Lakers star Shaquille O'Neal.

Adjusting to the NBA was no problem for Yao. He has he averaged 13.5 points, 8.2 rebounds, and 1.74 blocks to make the NBA All-Rookie First Team.

Last season, he increased his averages to 17.5 points, 9.0 rebounds, and 1.9 blocks to lead the Rockets to the playoffs for the first time since the 1998–99 season. He also shot 55.2 percent from the floor.

Both of Yao's parents played basketball for the Chinese National Team. Before being drafted by the Rockets, Yao played for the Shanghai Sharks, a club team owned by the Chinese government and private industry.

DID YOU KNOW?
That in China last names come first so in America Yao Ming would be called Ming Yao.

YAO BY THE NUMBERS 2003–04 SEASON: POINTS: 17.5 – ASSISTS: 1.5 – REBOUNDS: 9.0 – BLOCKS: 1.9

DIRK NOWITZKI

DALLAS MAVERICKS

BORN: 6/19/1978
HEIGHT: 7-0
WEIGHT: 245

THE GERMAN SENSATION

No one would be surprised if one of the best soccer players in the world was from Germany, but a basketball player? Meet Dallas Mavericks forward Dirk Nowitzki.

Now an NBA All-Star, Dirk has averaged 20.4 points and 8.3 rebounds in six NBA seasons. Born in Wurzburg, Germany, Dirk, like most German kids played soccer, but in 1992 when the United States Dream Team played in the Olympics, fourteen-year-old Dirk became fascinated with basketball.

He wanted to be like Chicago Bulls star Scottie Pippen. So he worked on his game constantly, the way he had heard American kids did, and the way many of his friends worked at soccer.

By the time he reached college age, Dirk had grown to 7 feet and had led DJK Wurzburg to a title in the German Bundesliga, Germany's professional basketball league.

Although he was a member of the German Junior National Team, Dirk didn't really catch the attention of NBA scouts until he participated in the 1998 Hoops Summit.

Playing against some of the best high school players in the United States, Dirk scored 33 to lead the team of international players to a surprise victory over the United States. Later that summer, Dirk was drafted ninth overall by the Milwaukee Bucks but was immediately traded to Dallas.

DID YOU KNOW?

Dirk enjoys reading and playing the saxophone in his spare time.

NOWITZKI BY THE NUMBERS ▶ 2003–04 SEASON: POINTS: 21.8 – REBOUNDS: 8.7 – BLOCKS: 1.35 – FREE THROWS: 87.7 %

JERMAINE O'NEAL

FORWARD/CENTER

INDIANA PACERS

BORN: 10/13/1978

HEIGHT: 6-11

WEIGHT: 242

SCHOOL: EAU CLAIRE HIGH SCHOOL (SOUTH CAROLINA)

PATIENCE IS A VIRTUE

The 1996 NBA Draft featured an amazing pool of talent — players like Ray Allen, Kobe Bryant, Allen Iverson, Stephon Marbury, and Shareef Abdur-Rahim — all of whom quickly developed into top stars in the league. But superstar status didn't come nearly as fast for Jermaine O'Neal.

Jermaine entered the draft right out of high school and was selected by the Portland Trail Blazers. But for the first four years of his career positive highlights were few and far between for the young center. His highest average during that time was 4.5 points in 1997–98.

Before the start of the 2000–01 season, Portland traded him to the Indiana Pacers. In Indiana, Jermaine started 80 games and averaged 12.9 points and 9.8 rebounds. He was named 2000–01 Most Improved Player and keeps getting better. In four seasons with the Pacers, Jermaine has made three All-Star Teams. He's averaged more than 20 points and 10 rebounds in each of the last two seasons.

It took a little time, but Jermaine has arrived. At 25, he has established himself as one of the top players in the league. He is the focal point of a Pacers team that should keep challenging for the NBA title for the foreseeable future.

DID YOU KNOW?

When Jermaine made his professional debut on December 5, 1995, he became the youngest player in league history at the age of 18 years, 1 month, and 22 days.

O'NEAL BY THE NUMBERS ◇ 2003–04 SEASON: POINTS: 20.1 – REBOUNDS: 10.09 BLOCKS: 10.0 – ASSISTS: 2.1

SHAQUILLE O'NEAL

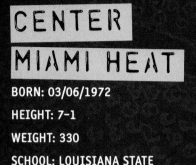

CENTER

MIAMI HEAT

BORN: 03/06/1972

HEIGHT: 7-1

WEIGHT: 330

SCHOOL: LOUISIANA STATE

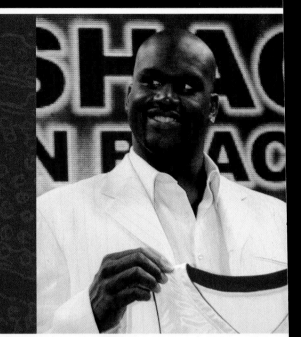

SHAQ IN BLACK

The balance of power has shifted. That's what happened when Shaquille O'Neal, the NBA's most dominant player, was traded to the Miami Heat from the Los Angeles Lakers. After thrilling fans for eight seasons and bringing three NBA titles to Los Angeles, O'Neal hopes to bring his championship touch to Miami.

The Heat was more than willing to step in and offer Shaq a new home. And why not? It's not every day that an NBA team gets to trade for a force of nature, and because of his size and power, that's exactly what Shaquille is when he steps onto the court. Acquiring Shaq, who is a three-time NBA Finals MVP, immediately changes the Heat from a developing team to a challenger for the Eastern Conference Championship.

"I feel absolutely blessed to be President of the Miami Heat," Pat Riley said on the day Shaq was acquired. "Players like Shaquille don't come around but once in a generation or once in a lifetime."

No player has a greater ability to change a game than Shaq, because he is simply unstoppable around the basket. Since he entered the NBA in 1992 with the Orlando Magic, Shaq has never averaged less than 21 points and 10.5 rebounds. His career averages are 27.1 points and 12.1 rebounds.

Named one of the 50 Greatest Players in NBA history in 1996, Shaq is determined to live up to that honor by bringing Miami its first NBA title. Who is going to stop him?

DID YOU KNOW?

Shaquille has released five rap albums, *Shaq Diesel, Shaq Fu: Da Return, You Can't Stop the Reign, Respect,* and a greatest hits album; and starred in the movies *Blue Chips, Kazaam,* and *Steel.*

O'NEAL BY THE NUMBERS 2003–04 SEASON: POINTS: 21.5 – REBOUNDS: 11.5 BLOCKS: 2.49 – FIELD GOAL % – 58.4

BEN WALLACE

FORWARD/CENTER

DETROIT PISTONS

BORN: 09/10/1974

HEIGHT: 6-9

WEIGHT: 240

SCHOOL: VIRGINIA UNION

HAIR-RAISING PLAY

Ben Wallace took the long road to the NBA.

First, Ben, who played at NCAA Division II Virginia Union University, wasn't selected in the 1996 NBA Draft. He went to the Italian Basketball League before making the Washington Bullets' (now the Wizards) roster as a free agent and played three seasons there but was traded to the Orlando Magic in 1999.

A year later, he was traded from the Magic to the Detroit Pistons. In the Motor City, "Big Ben" found a home and his niche as an NBA player. Ben has made himself into one of the most dominant players in the league by becoming a dominant rebounder and defender. For his career, Wallace has averaged just 6.1 points but he has pulled down 10.4 rebounds a game. He's averaged more than 3.0 blocks a game for the past three seasons, making him one of the most feared shot blockers in the NBA.

Ben is a two-time NBA Defensive Player of the Year and during the 2001–02 season became just the fourth player to lead the league in rebounds and blocked shots. In 2004, he helped the Pistons upset the Los Angeles Lakers for 2004 NBA Championship. It's just the beginning for Ben and the Pistons.

DID YOU KNOW?

Ben attended the same college as former New York Knicks and Chicago Bulls star Charles Oakley and in 2003 became the first undrafted player to ever start in an NBA All-Star Game.

WALLACE BY THE NUMBERS> 2003–04 SEASON: POINTS: 9.5 – REBOUNDS: 12.4 – BLOCKS: 3.04

JUST THE FACTS:

REGULAR SEASON POINTS PER GAME

	Player	G	FG	FT	P	PG
1.	Tracy McGrady (Orlando Magic)	67	653	398	1,878	28.0
2.	Peja Stojakovic (Sacramento Kings)	81	665	394	1,964	24.2
2.	Kevin Garnett (Minnesota Timberwolves)	82	804	368	1,987	24.2
4.	Kobe Bryant (Los Angeles Lakers)	65	516	454	1,557	24.0
5.	Paul Pierce (Boston Celtics)	80	602	517	1,836	23.0
6.	Baron Davis (New Orleans Hornets)	67	554	237	1,532	22.9
7.	Vince Carter (Toronto Raptors)	73	608	336	1,645	22.5
8.	Tim Duncan (San Antonio Spurs)	69	592	352	1,538	22.3
9.	Dirk Nowitzki (Dallas Mavericks)	77	605	371	1,680	21.8
10.	Michael Redd (Milwaukee Bucks)	82	633	383	1,776	21.7

2003-04

REGULAR SEASON ROOKIE LEADERS: POINTS PER GAME

	Player	G	FG	FT	PTS	PPG
1.	Carmelo Anthony (Denver Nuggets)	82	624	408	1,725	21.0
2.	LeBron James (Cleveland Cavaliers)	79	622	347	1,654	20.9
3.	Dwyane Wade (Miami Heat)	61	371	233	991	16.2
4.	Kirk Hinrich (Chicago Bulls)	76	318	135	915	12.0
5.	Chris Bosh (Toronto Raptors)	75	327	202	861	11.5
6.	Jarvis Hayes (Washington Wizards)	70	278	77	673	9.6
7.	Josh Howard (Dallas Mavericks)	67	229	97	575	8.6
8.	Marquis Daniels (Dallas Mavericks)	56	203	60	477	8.5
9.	Leandro Barbosa (Phoenix Suns)	70	210	47	550	7.9
10.	Udonis Haslem (Miami Heat)	75	205	140	550	7.3

2003-04

REGULAR SEASON POINTS

	Player	G	FG	FT	P	PG
1.	Kevin Garnett (Minnesota Timberwolves)	82	804	368	1,987	24.2
2.	Peja Stojakovic (Sacramento Kings)	81	665	394	1,964	24.2
3.	Tracy McGrady (Orlando Magic)	67	653	398	1,878	28.0
4.	Paul Pierce (Boston Celtics)	80	602	517	1,836	23.0
5.	Michael Redd (Milwaukee Bucks)	82	633	383	1,776	21.7
6.	Carmelo Anthony (Denver Nuggets)	82	624	408	1,725	21.0
7.	Dirk Nowitzki (Dallas Mavericks)	77	605	371	1,680	21.8
8.	LeBron James (Cleveland Cavaliers)	79	622	347	1,654	20.9
9.	Vince Carter (Toronto Raptors)	73	608	336	1,645	22.5
10.	Stephon Marbury (New York Knicks)	81	598	356	1,639	20.2

2003-04

REGULAR SEASON ROOKIE LEADERS: POINTS

	Player	G	FG	FT	PPG	PTS
1.	Carmelo Anthony (Denver Nuggets)	82	624	408	21.0	1,725
2.	LeBron James (Cleveland Cavaliers)	79	622	347	20.9	1,654
3.	Dwyane Wade (Miami Heat)	61	371	233	16.2	991
4.	Kirk Hinrich (Chicago Bulls)	76	318	135	12.0	915
5.	Chris Bosh (Toronto Raptors)	75	327	202	11.5	861
6.	Jarvis Hayes (Washington Wizards)	70	278	77	9.6	673
7.	Josh Howard (Dallas Mavericks)	67	229	97	8.6	575
8.	Raul Lopez (Utah Jazz)	82	223	101	7.0	572
9.	Leandro Barbosa (Phoenix Suns)	70	210	47	7.9	550
9.	Udonis Haslem (Miami Heat)	75	205	140	7.3	550
11.	Chris Kaman (Los Angeles Clippers)	82	200	99	6.1	499